HAL•LEONARD®
GUITAR PLAY-ALONG

AUDIO ACCESS INCLUDED

Slide Guitar HITS

CONTENTS

T0079961

PLAYBACK+
Speed • Pitch • Balance • Loop

To access audio visit:
www.halleonard.com/mylibrary

Enter Code
4301-6013-2087-0671

ISBN 978-1-4234-6870-7

HAL•LEONARD®

Visit Hal Leonard Online at
www.halleonard.com

Contact us:
Hal Leonard
7777 West Bluemound Road
Milwaukee, WI 53213
Email: info@halleonard.com

In Europe, contact:
Hal Leonard Europe Limited
42 Wigmore Street
Marylebone, London, W1U 2RN
Email: info@halleonardeurope.com

In Australia, contact:
Hal Leonard Australia Pty. Ltd.
4 Lentara Court
Cheltenham, Victoria, 3192 Australia
Email: info@halleonard.com.au

Bad to the Bone

Words and Music by George Thorogood

Open G tuning:
(low to high) D-G-D-G-B-D

Intro
Moderately ♩ = 100

Verse

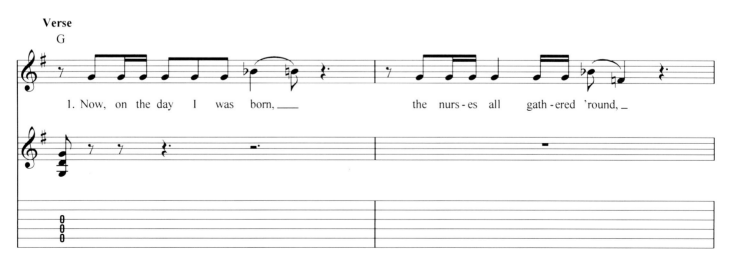

1. Now, on the day I was born, ___ the nurs-es all gath-ered 'round, ___

and they gazed___ in wide won - der   at the joy___ they had found.___

The head nurse   spoke up,   said, "Leave___ this one a - lone."___

She could tell ___ right a - way _____   that I was bad   to the bone.

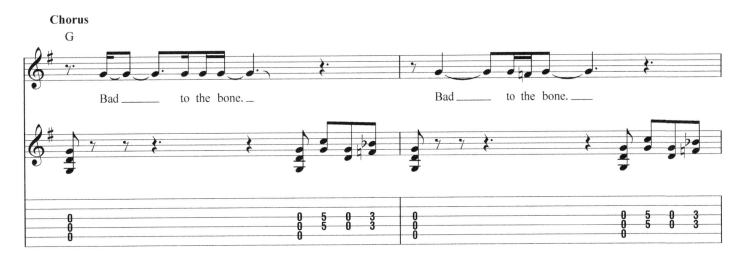

Chorus

G

Bad _____ to the bone. _   Bad _____ to the bone. __

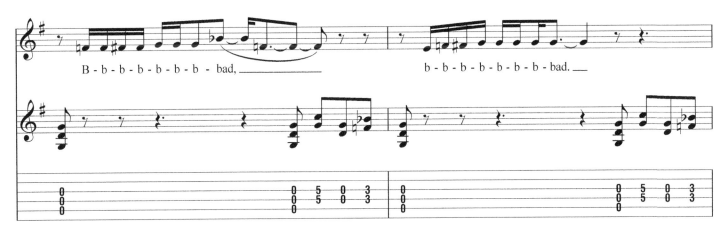

B - b - b - b - b - b - b - bad, _____   b - b - b - b - b - b - b - bad. __

B - b - b - b - b - b - bad, _____ bad _____ to the bone. _

% **Verse**

G

2. I broke a thou - sand hearts   be - fore I met you. __
3., 4. *See additional lyrics*

Gtr. tacet

I'll break a thou - sand more ba - by, _____   be - fore I am through. _

3

I wan-na be yours pret-ty ba - by,   yours and yours_ a - lone. _____

To Coda 1 ⊕

I'm here to tell ya __ hon - ey, __   that I'm bad   to the bone.

Chorus

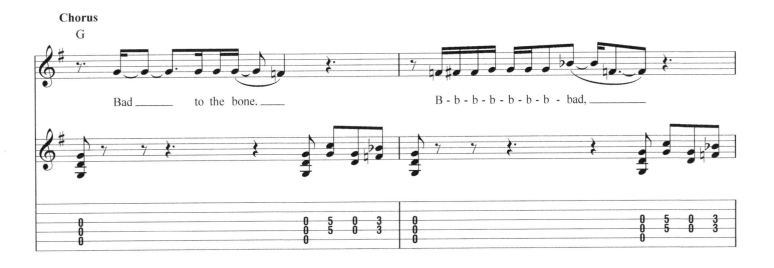

Bad _____ to the bone. _____

B - b - b - b - b - b - b - bad, _____

B - b - b - b - b - b - b - bad. _____

B - b - b - b - b - b - b - bad, _____

To Coda 2 ⊕

Guitar Solo

G

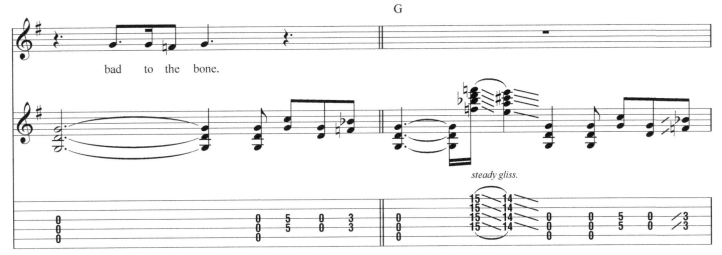

bad to the bone.

steady gliss.

let ring - - - - - - - - - - - -

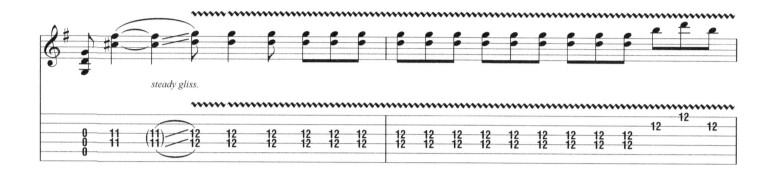

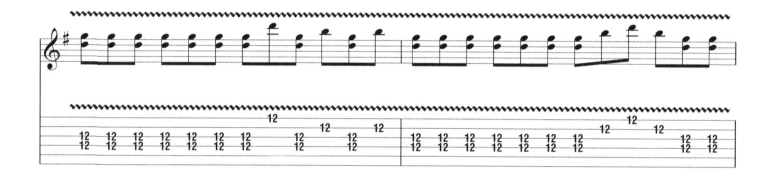

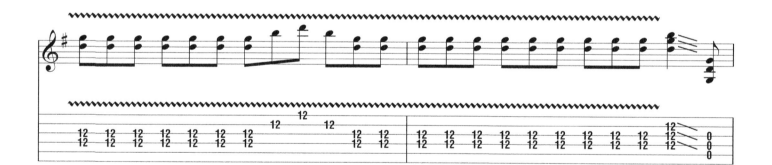

D.S. al Coda 1

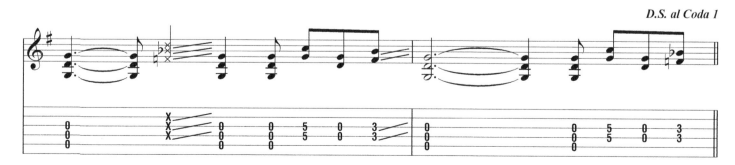

⊕ Coda 1

Chorus

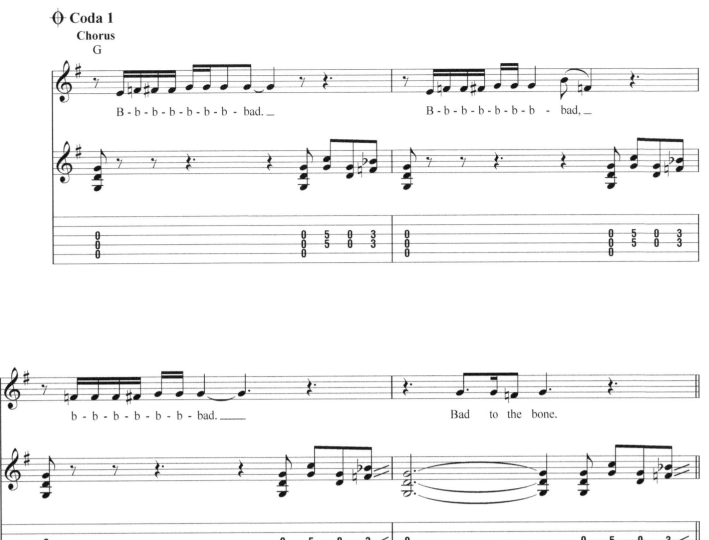

B - b - b - b - b - b - b - bad. _____   B - b - b - b - b - b - b - bad, _____

b - b - b - b - b - b - b - bad. _____   Bad   to   the   bone.

Saxophone Solo

G

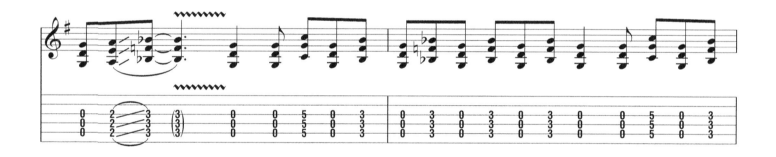

Guitar Solo

G

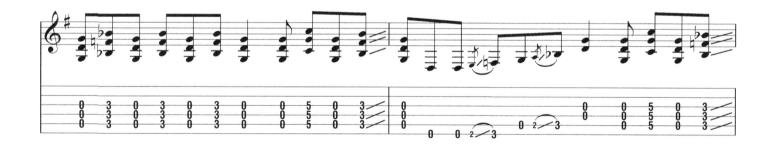

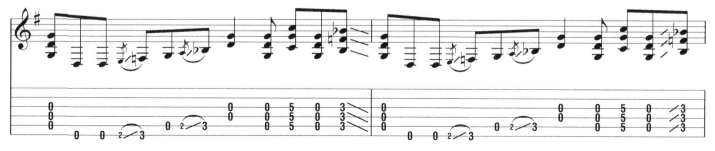

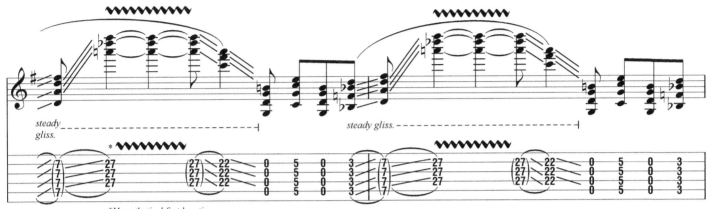

*Hypothetical fret location.

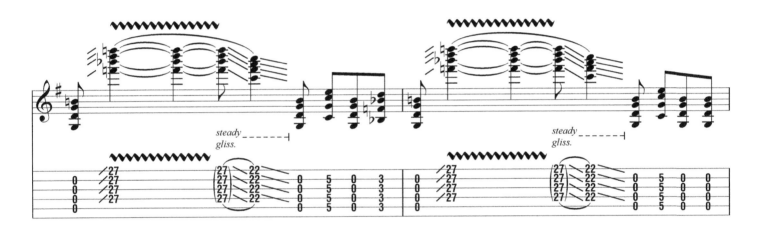

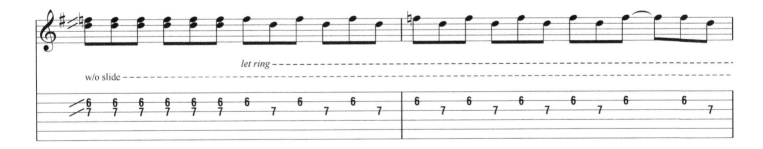

D.S. al Coda 2

⊕ Coda 2
Outro
G

Additional Lyrics

3. I make a rich woman beg,
   And I make a good woman steal.
   I make an old woman blush,
   And I make a young girl squeal.
   I wanna be yours pretty baby,
   Yours and yours alone.
   I'm here to tell ya honey,
   That I'm bad to the bone.

4. Now when I walk the streets,
   Kings and queens step aside.
   Every woman I meet,
   They all stay satisfied.
   I wanna tell ya pretty baby,
   What I see I make my own.
   And I'm here to tell ya honey,
   That I'm bad to the bone.

Free Bird

Words and Music by Allen Collins and Ronnie Van Zant

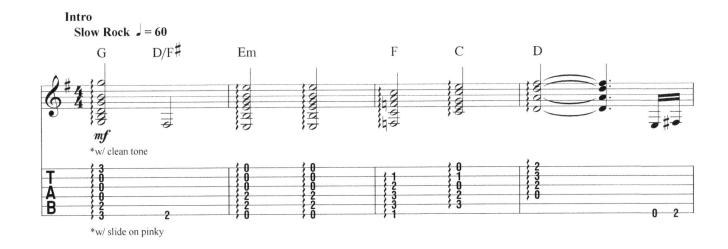

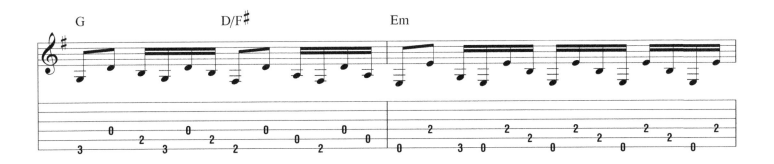

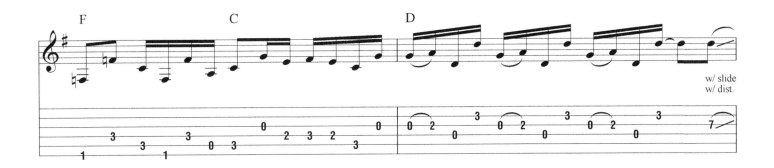

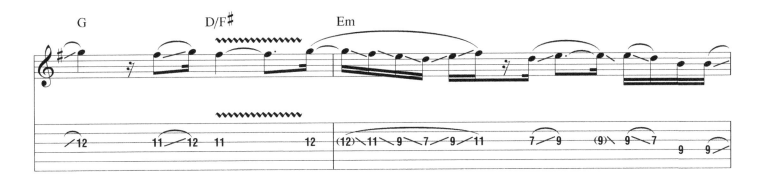

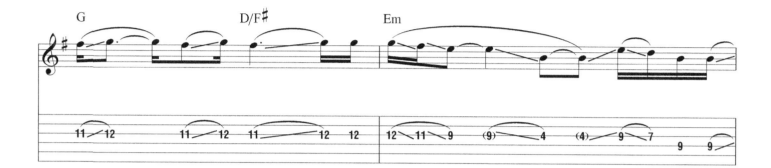

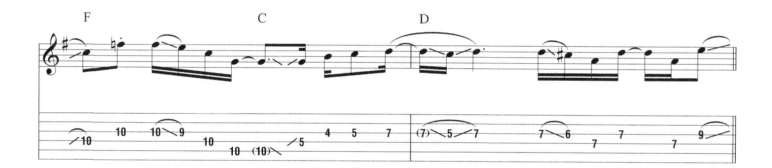

Verse

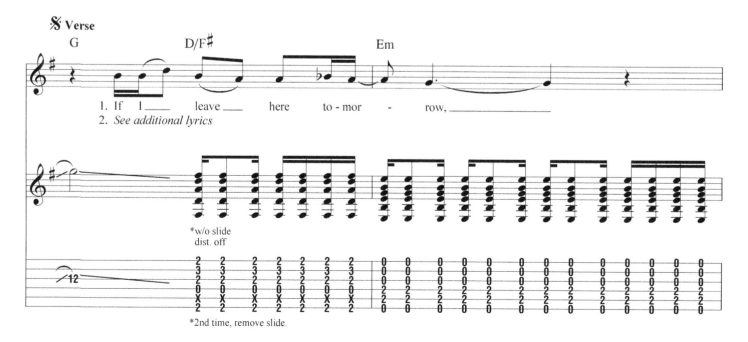

1. If I ___ leave ___ here to - mor - row, ___
2. *See additional lyrics*

*w/o slide
dist. off

*2nd time, remove slide.

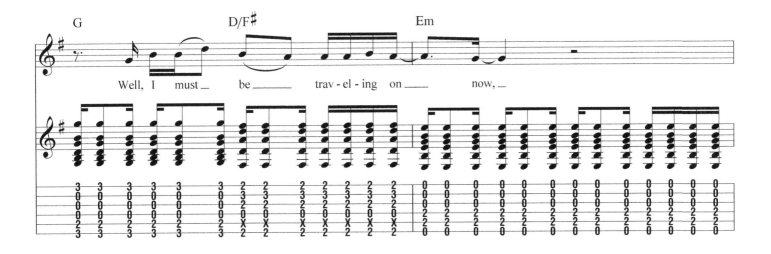

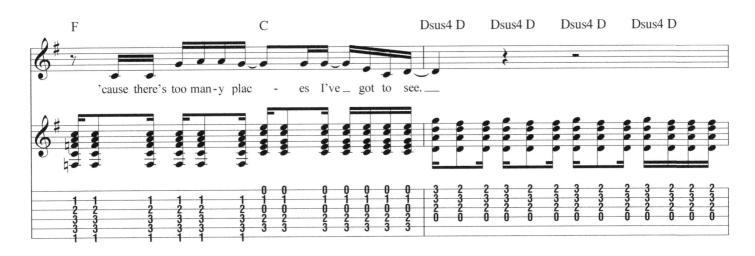

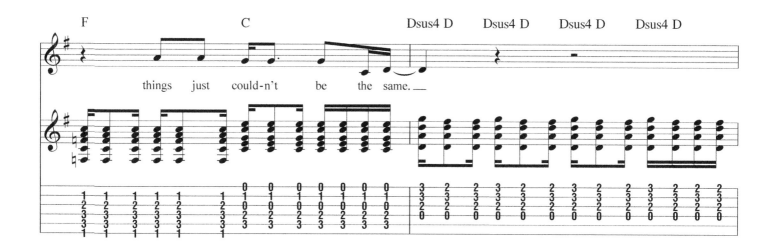

things just could-n't be the same. ___

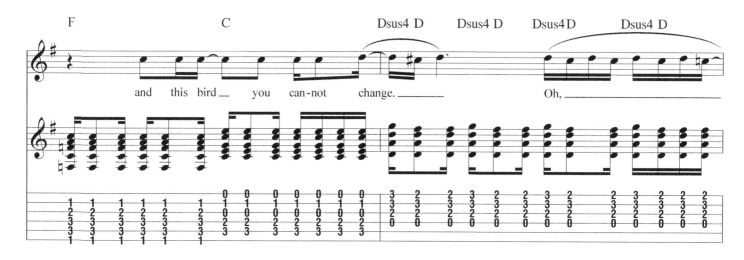

'Cause I'm as ___ free ___ as a bird ___ now, _

and this bird ___ you can-not change. _____ Oh,

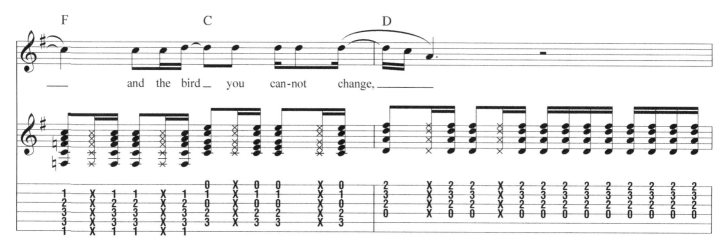

___ and the bird ___ you can-not change, _____

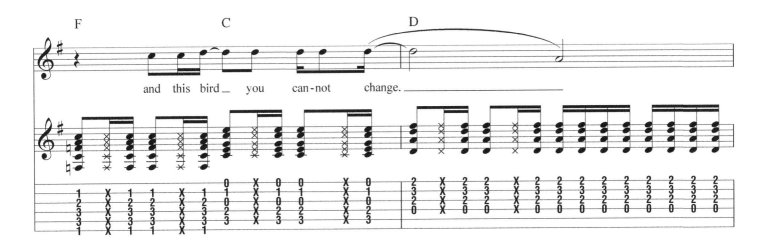

and this bird __ you can-not change. _____

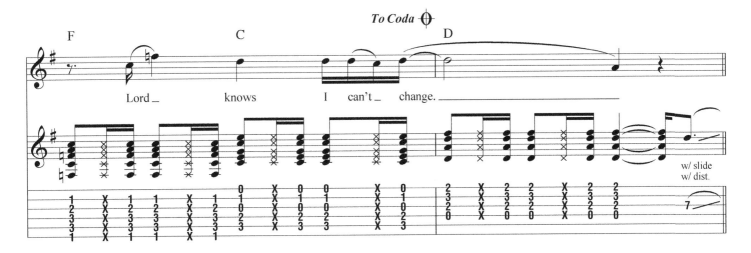

To Coda ⊕

Lord __ knows I can't __ change. _____

w/ slide
w/ dist.

Interlude

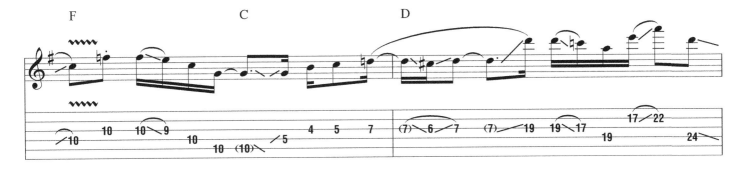

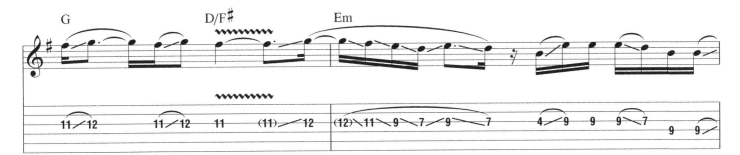

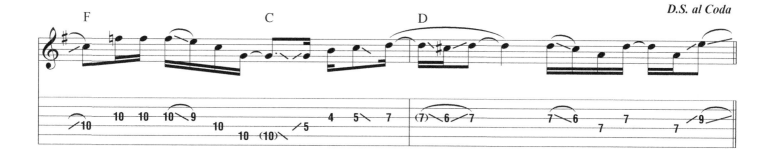

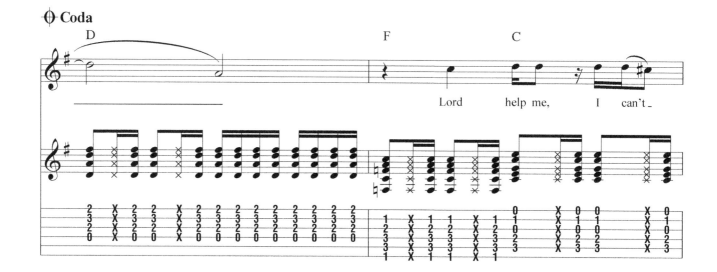

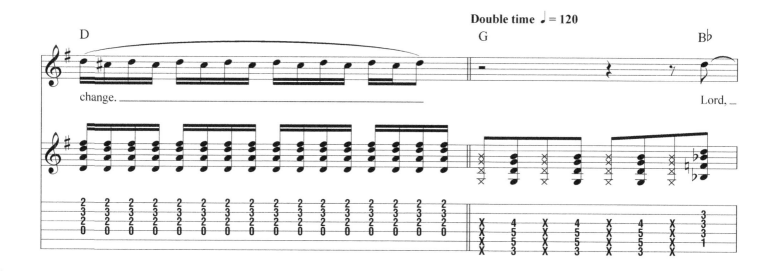

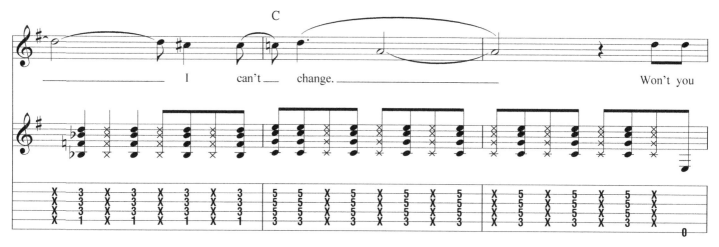

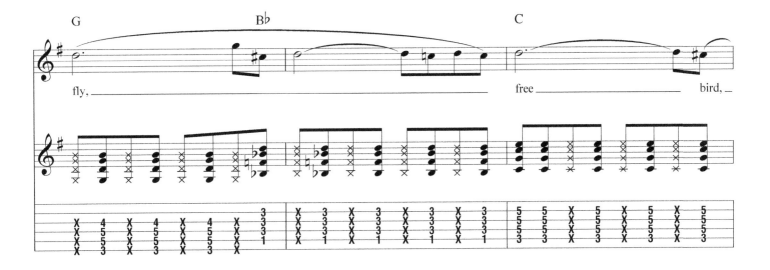

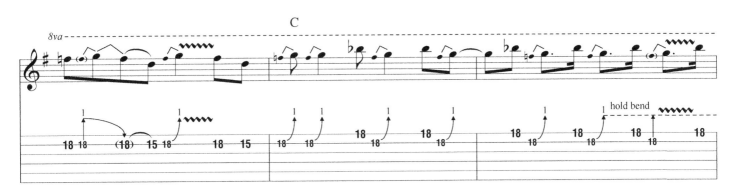

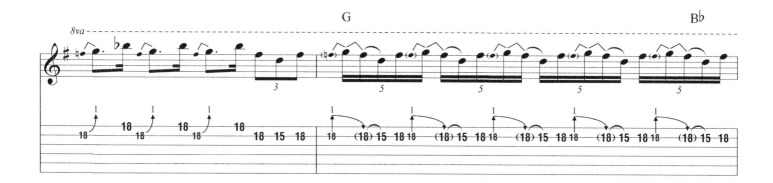

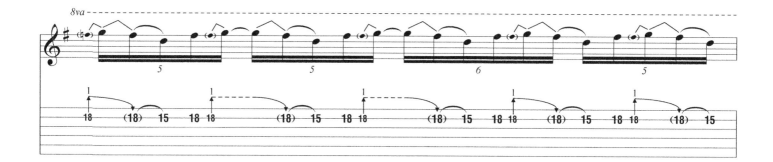

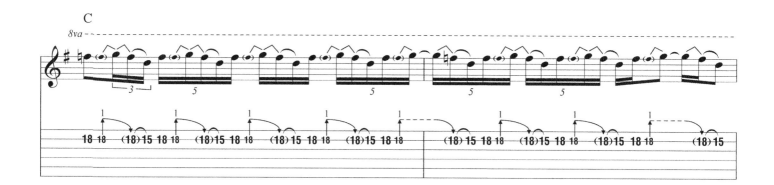

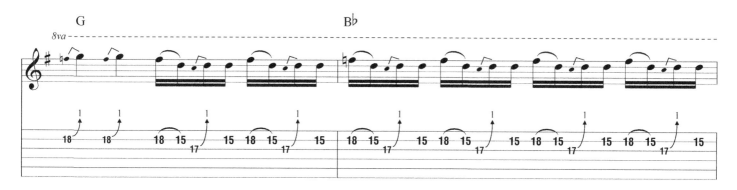

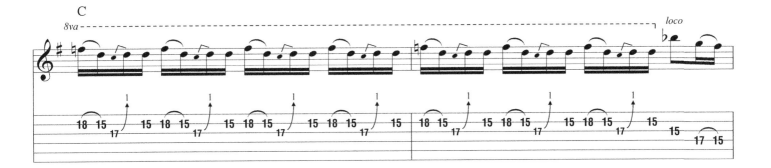

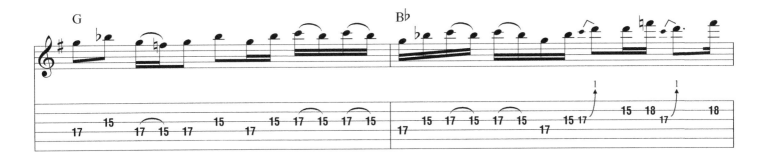

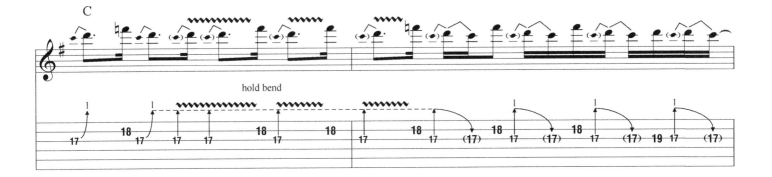

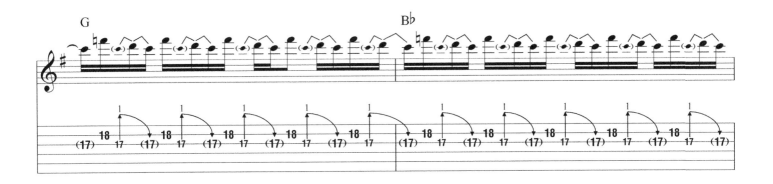

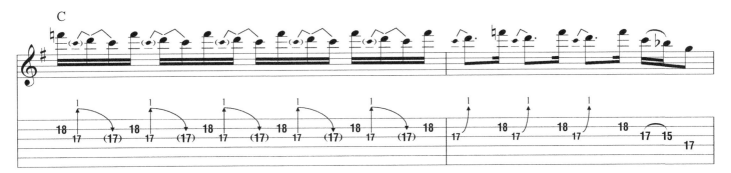

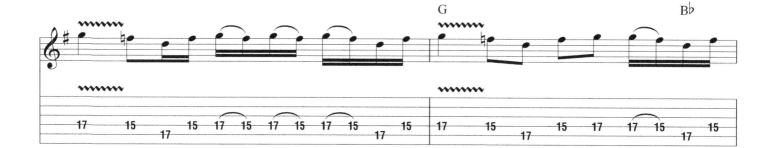

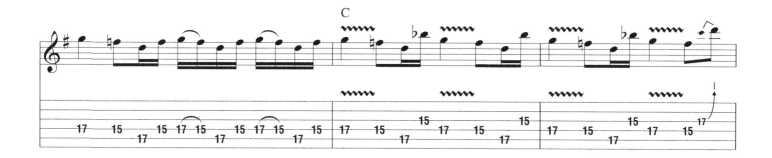

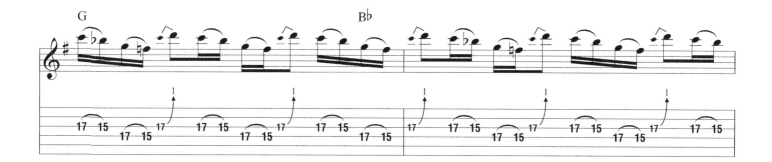

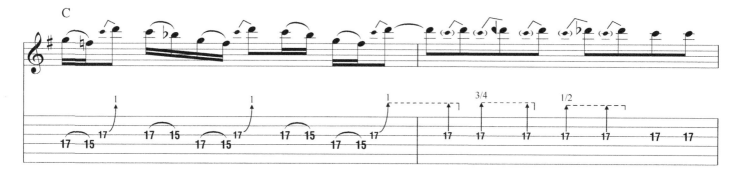

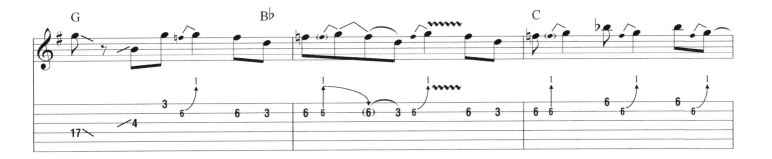

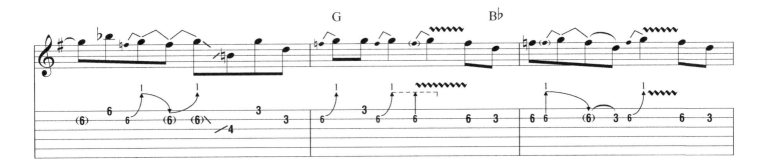

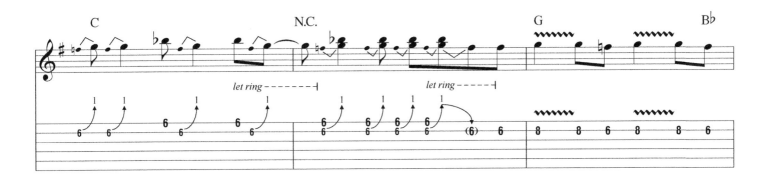

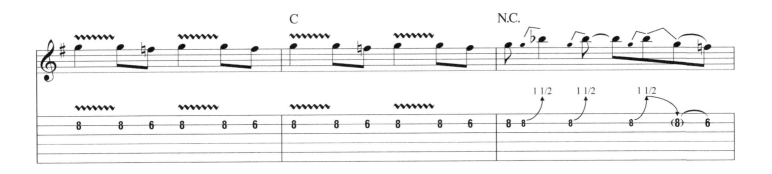

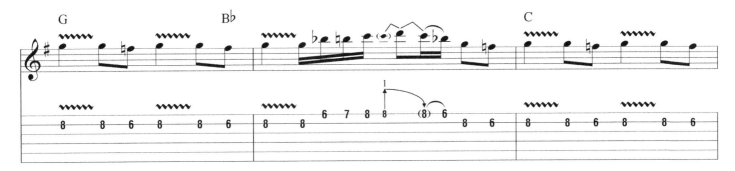

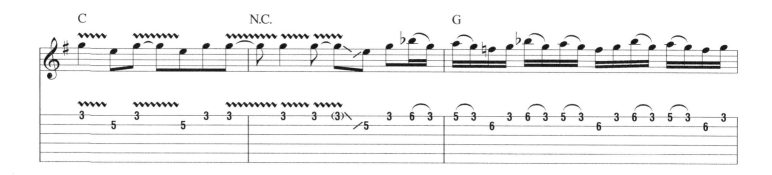

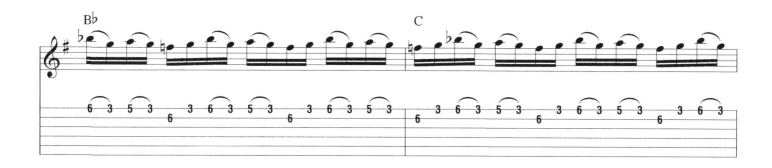

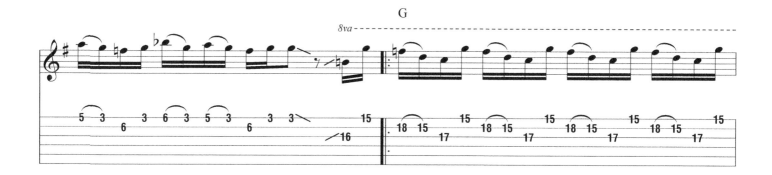

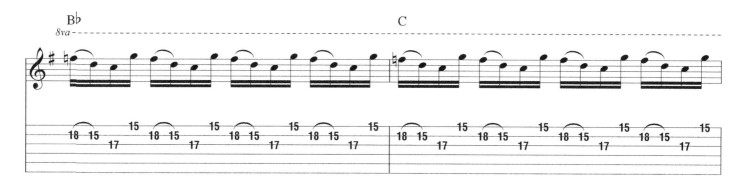

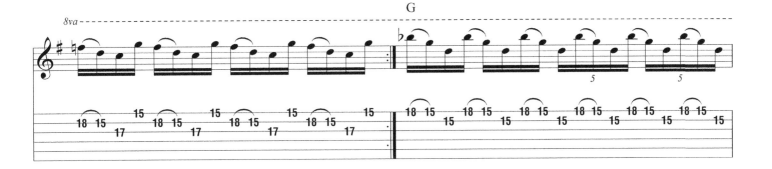

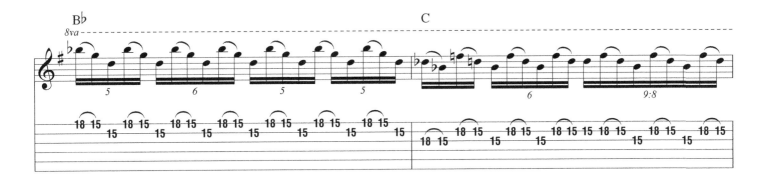

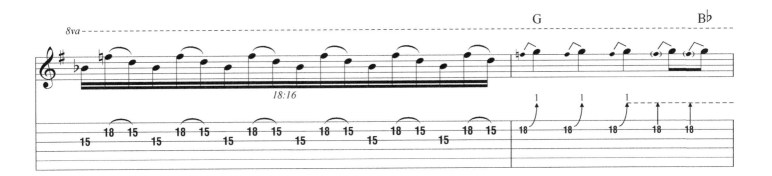

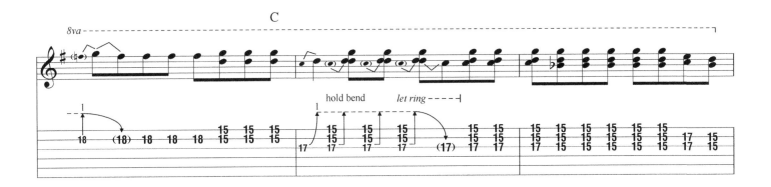

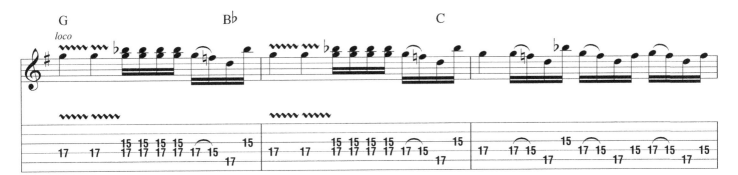

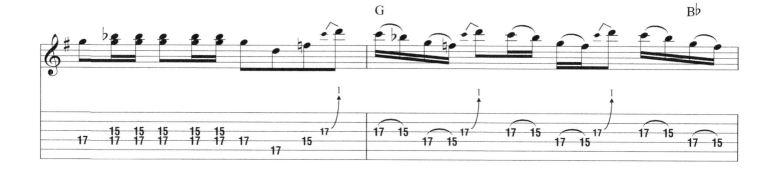

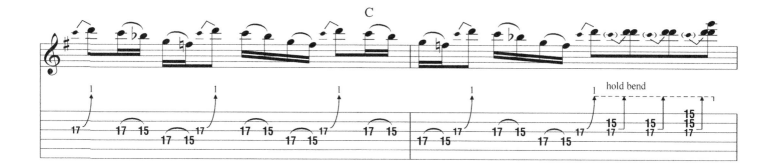

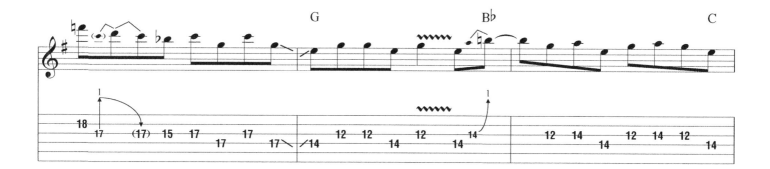

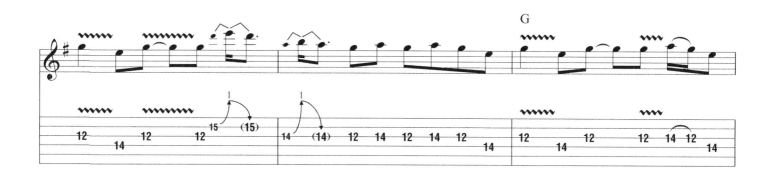

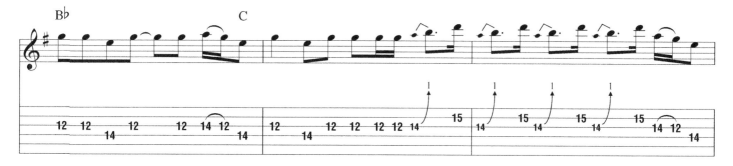

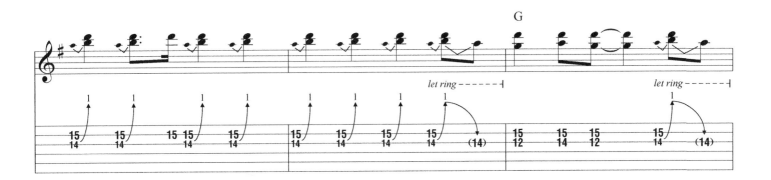

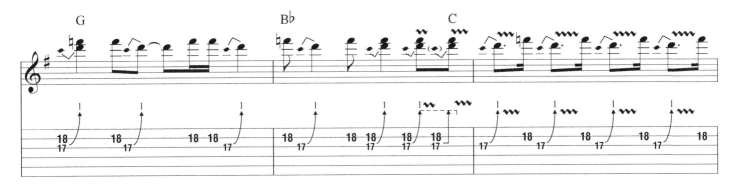

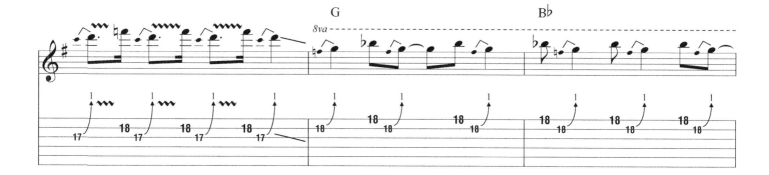

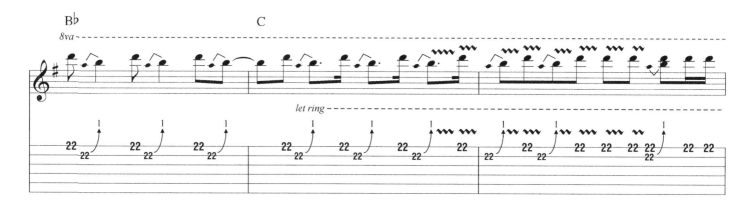

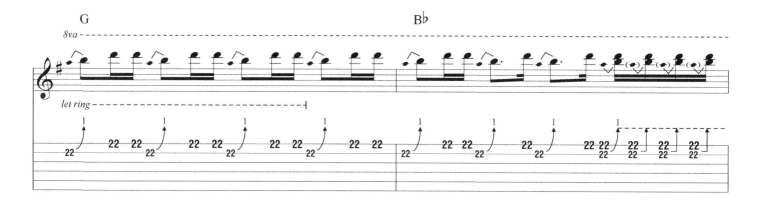

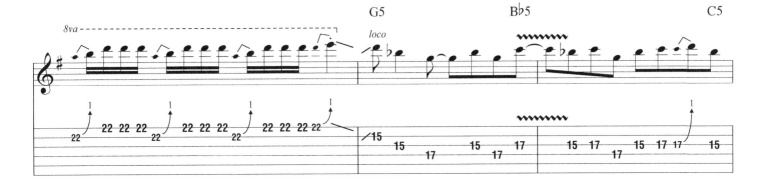

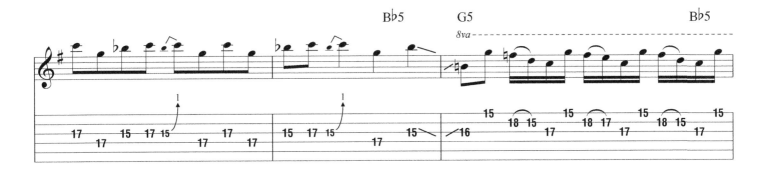

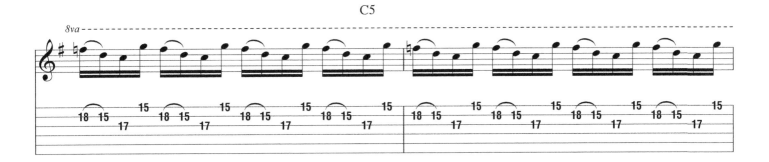

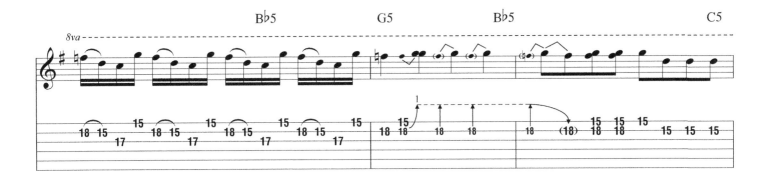

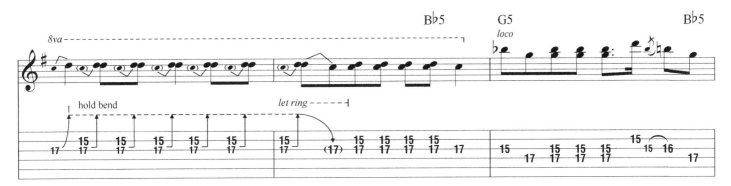

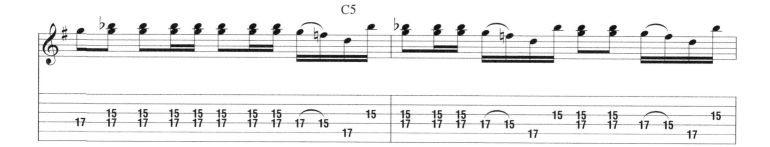

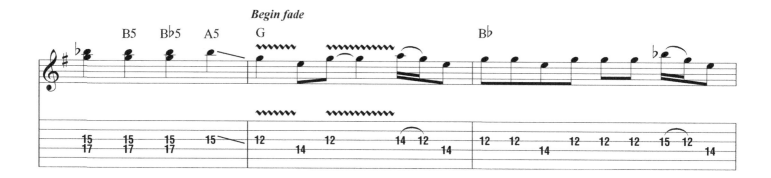

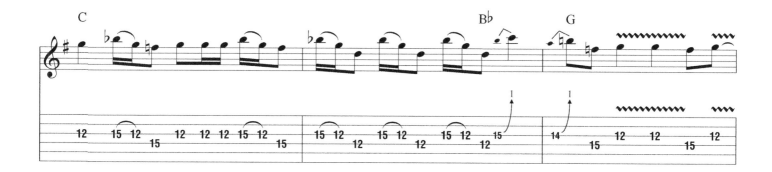

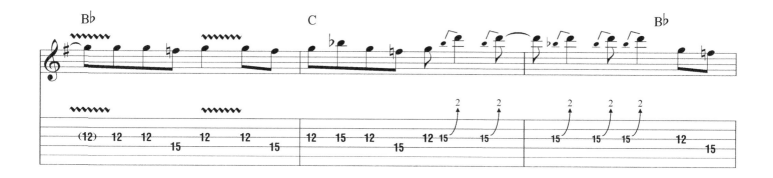

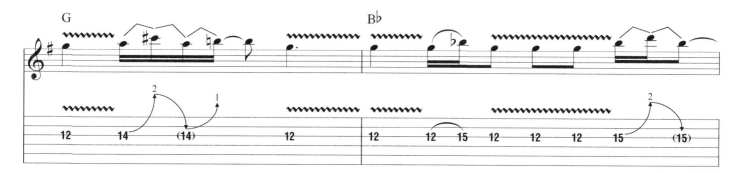

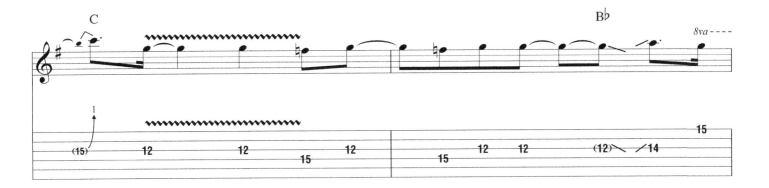

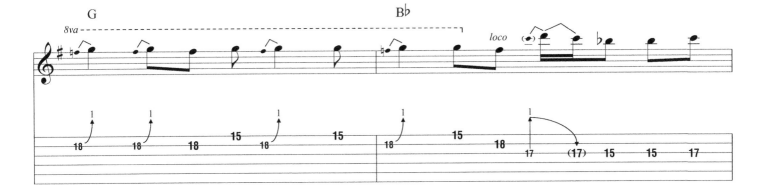

Fade out

Additional Lyrics

2. Bye bye, baby, it's been sweet now, yeah, yeah.
   Though this feelin' I can't change,
   A, please don't take it so badly,
   'Cause the Lord knows I'm to blame.
   But if I stay here with you, girl,
   Things just couldn't be the same.
   'Cause I'm as free as a bird now,
   And this bird you cannot change.
   Oh, and a bird you cannot change.
   And this bird you cannot change.
   Lord knows, I can't change.
   Lord help me, I can't change.

Layla

Words and Music by Eric Clapton and Jim Gordon

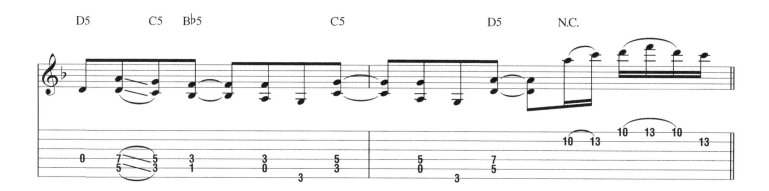

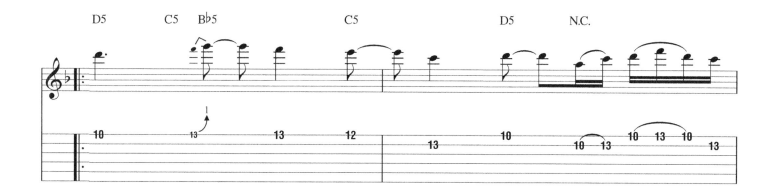

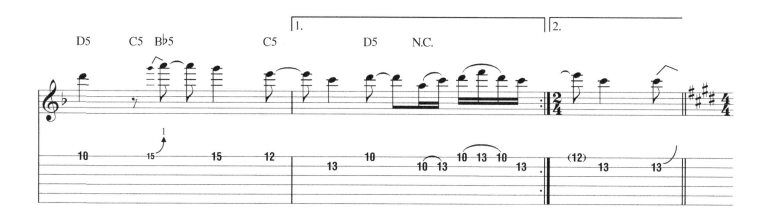

Chorus

You got me on__ my knees. __
la. _____
Lay -

I beg you, dar - lin', please, __ Lay - la, ____
la.) _____

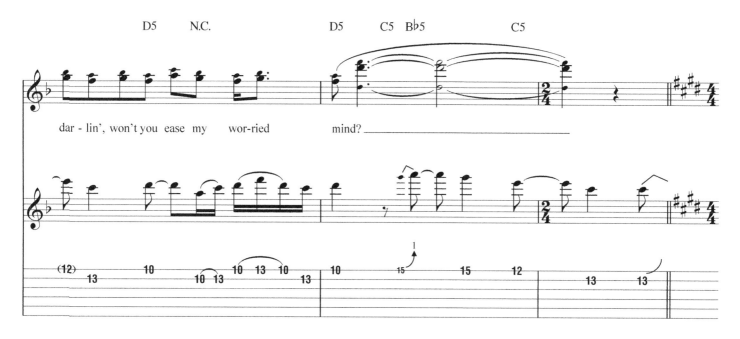

dar - lin', won't you ease my wor-ried mind? _____

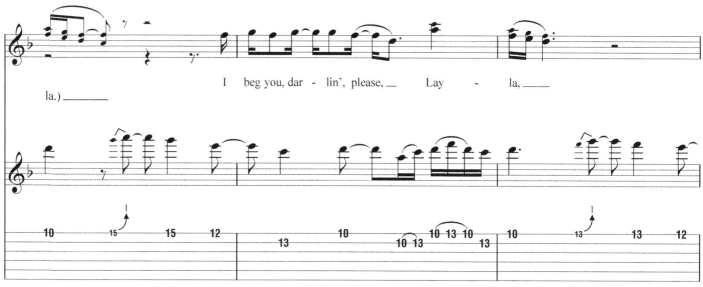

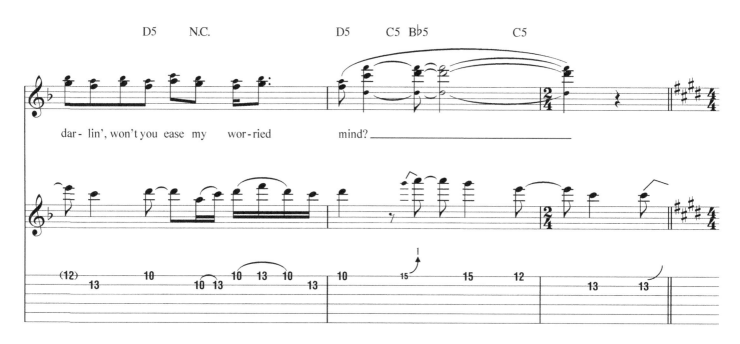

Chorus

You got me on ___ my knees. ___ Lay -

la. ____

I beg you, dar - lin', please, ___ Lay - la, ___

la.) ____

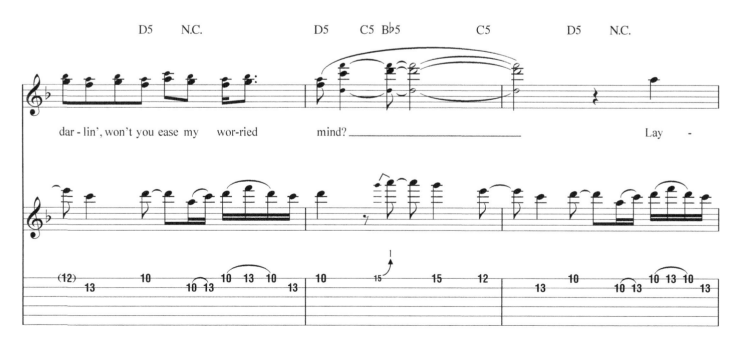

dar - lin', won't you ease my wor - ried mind? _____ Lay -

la, _____ you got me on __ my knees. __ Lay -
(Lay - la. _____)

I beg you, dar - lin', please. __ Lay - la, _____ (Whoa.) _
la.) _____

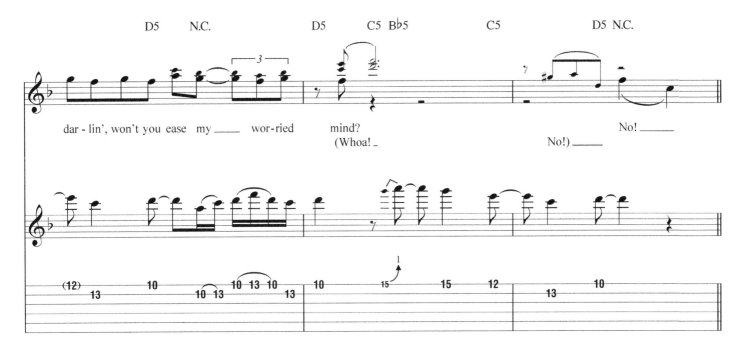

dar - lin', won't you ease my _____ wor - ried mind? No! _____
(Whoa! _ No!) _____

Guitar Solo

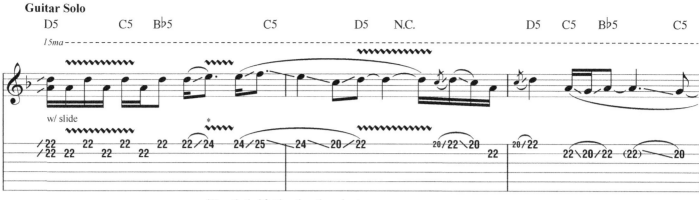

*Hypothetical fret locations throughout.

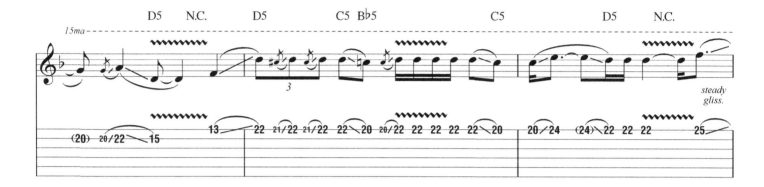

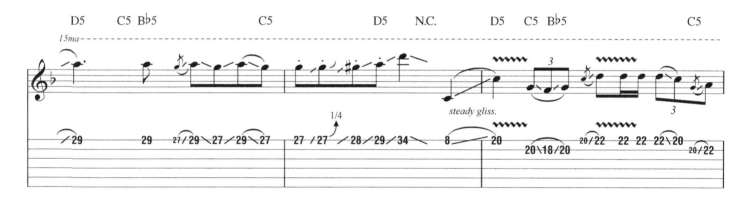

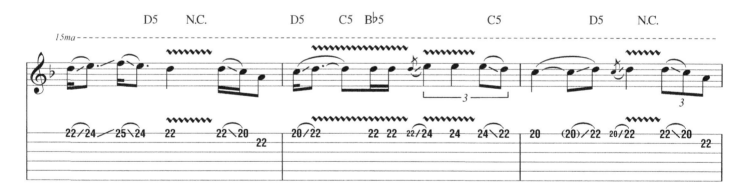

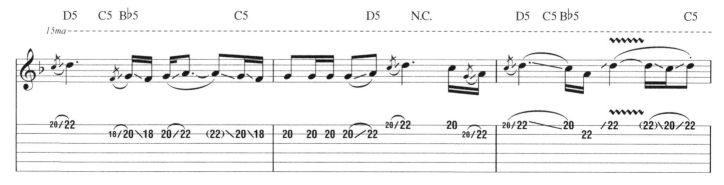

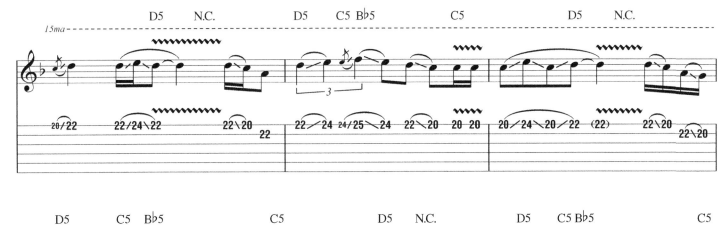

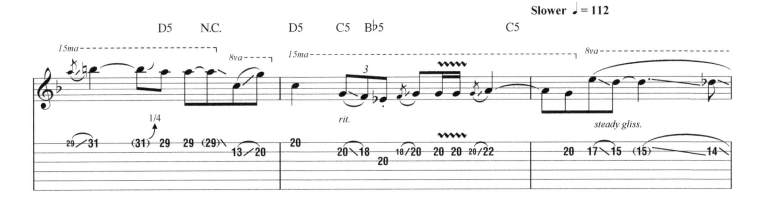

Interlude

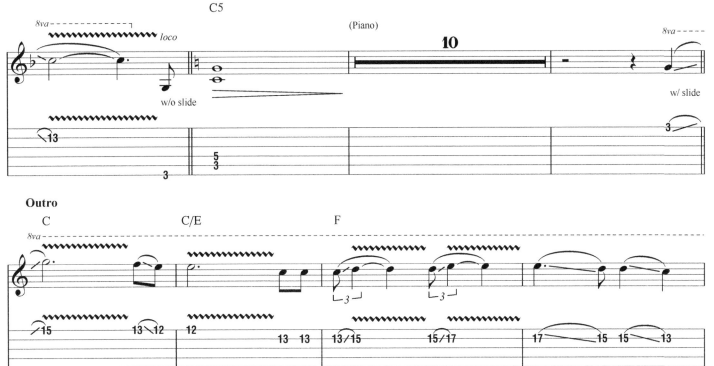

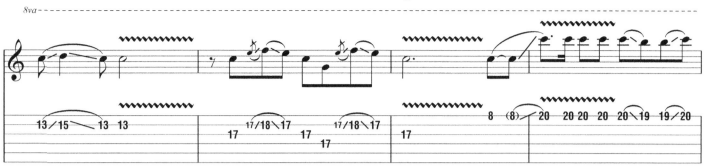

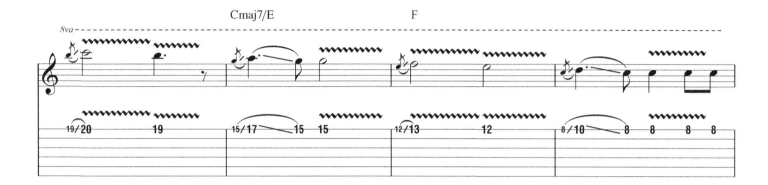

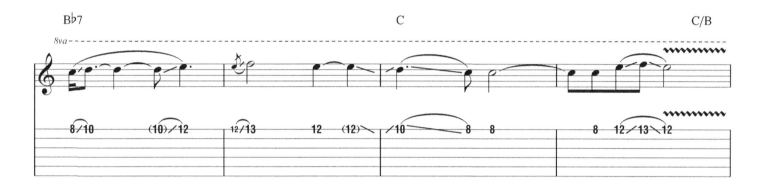

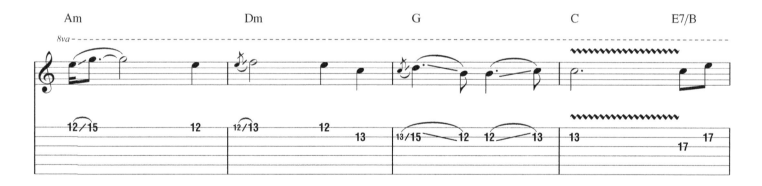

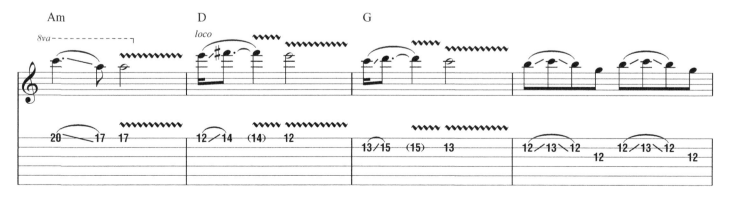

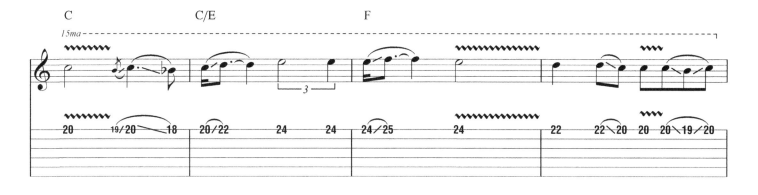

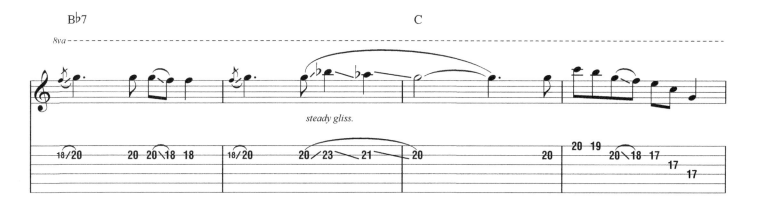

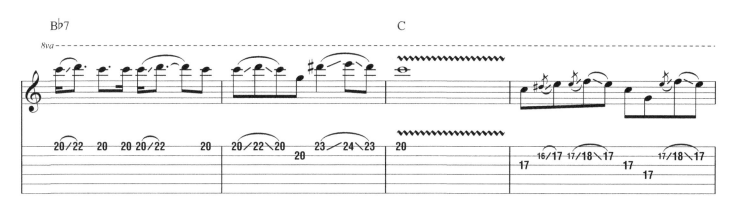

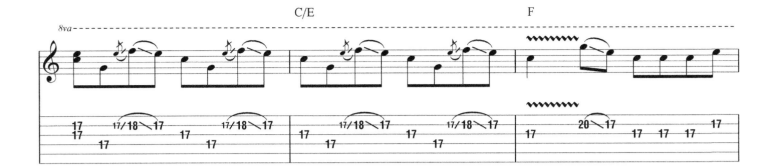

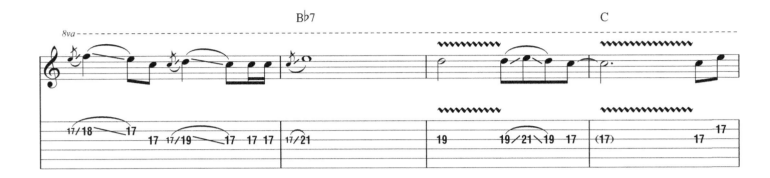

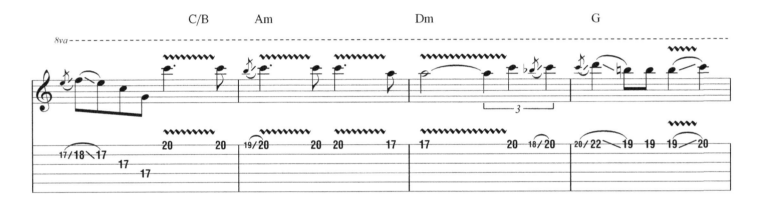

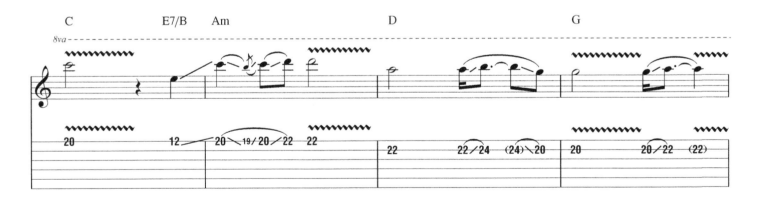

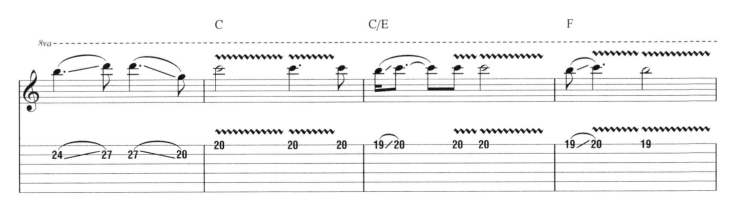

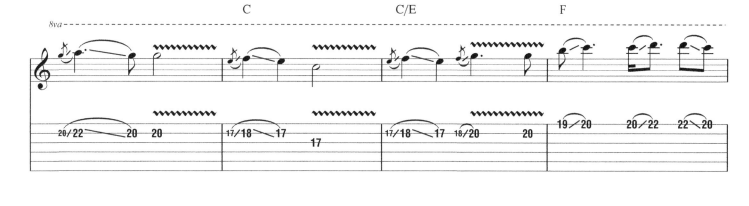

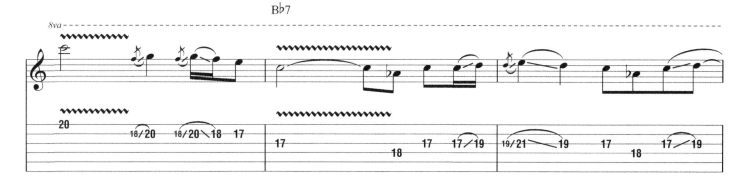

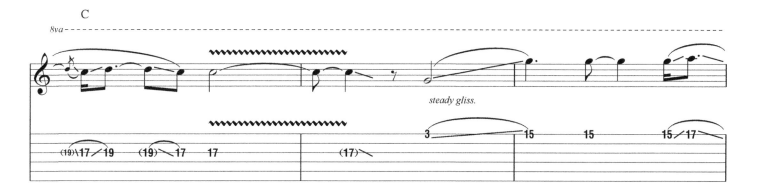

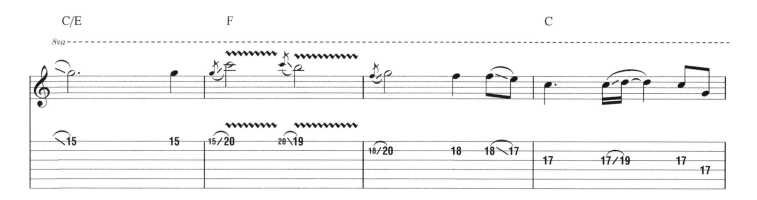

43

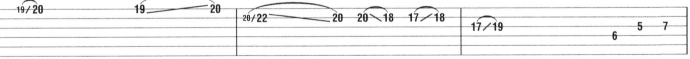

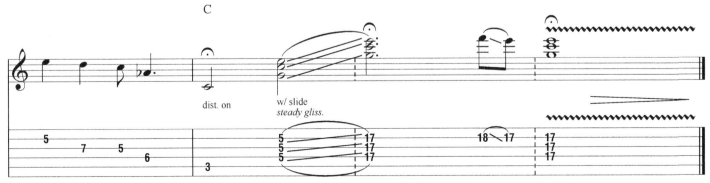

Tumbling Dice

Words and Music by Mick Jagger and Keith Richards

Open G tuning, capo IV:
(low to high) D-G-D-G-B-D

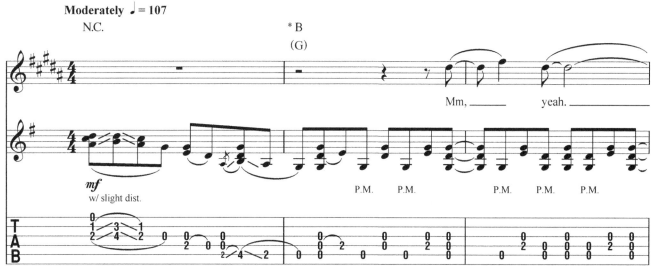

*Symbols in parentheses represent chord names respective to capoed guitar.
Symbols above reflect actual sounding chords. Capoed fret is "0" in tab.

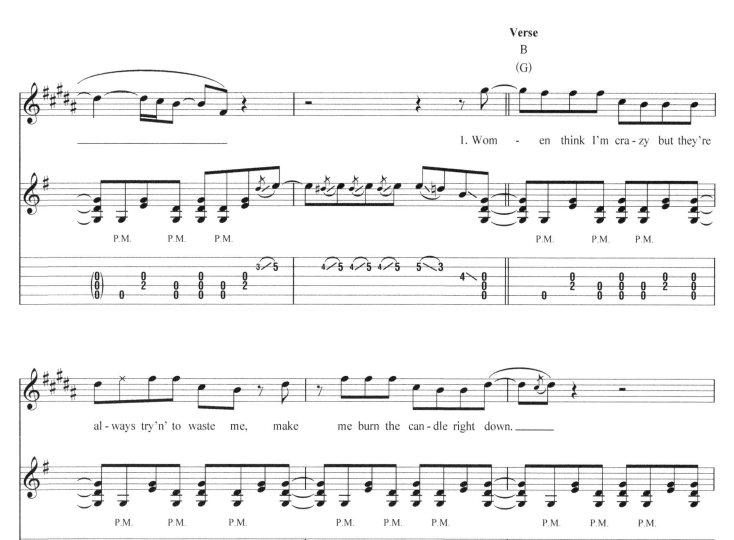

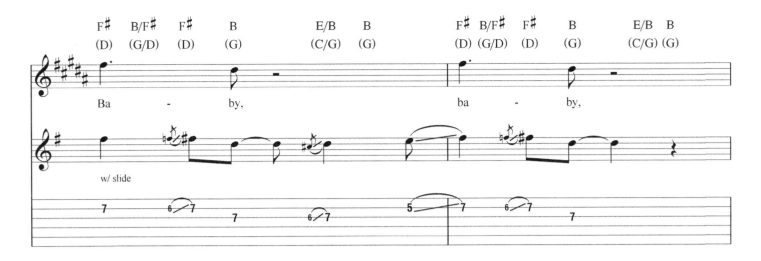

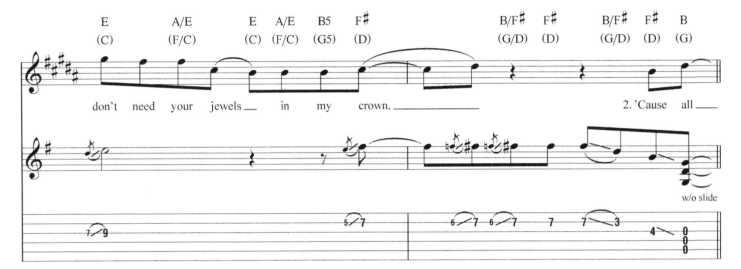

Verse

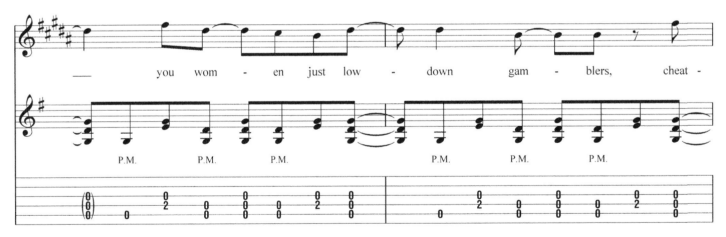

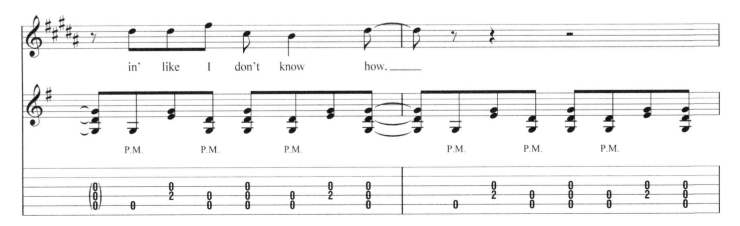

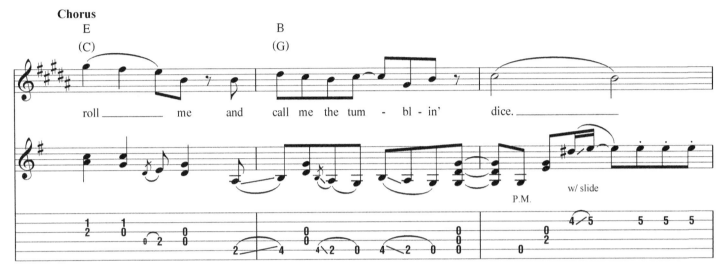

Chorus

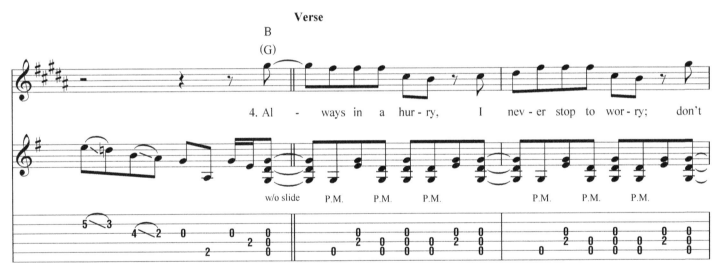

Verse

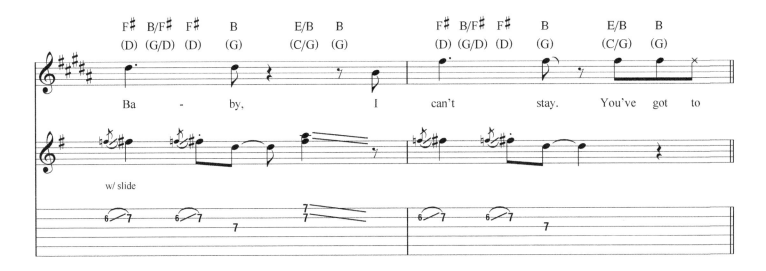

Chorus

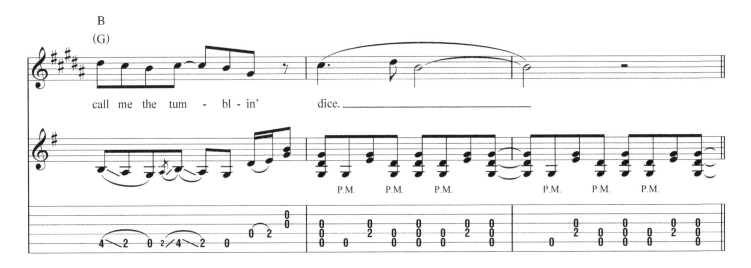

Guitar Solo

One Way Out

By Willie Williamson, Elmore James and Marshall Sehorn

Open E tuning:
(low to high) E-B-E-G#-B-E

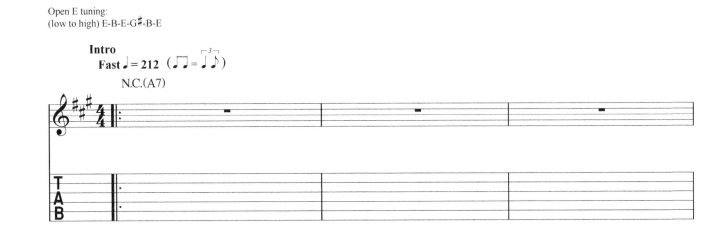

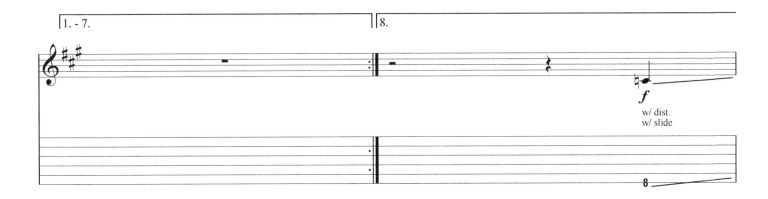

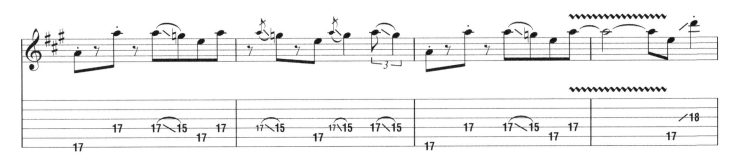

D7

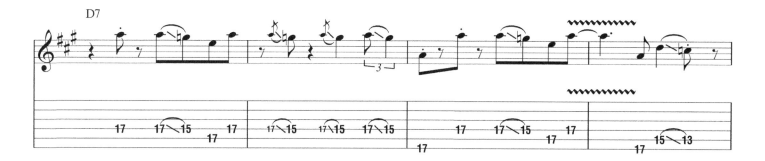

A7

E7   **D7**

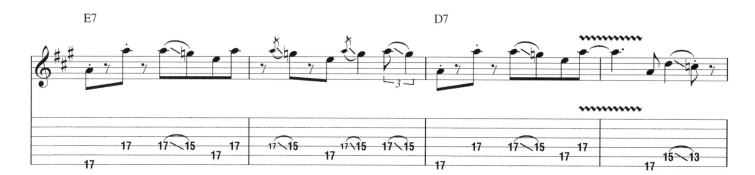

A7

1. Ain't but

Verse

A7

one way   out,___ ba - by.___   Lord, I   just___

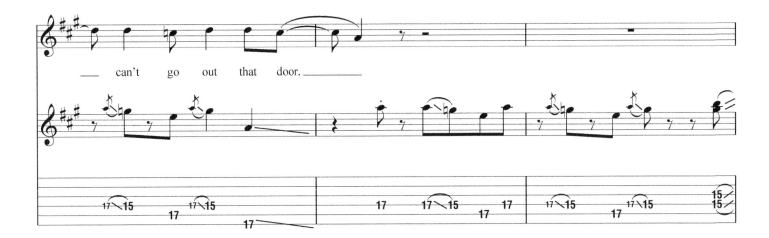

___ can't go out that door._____

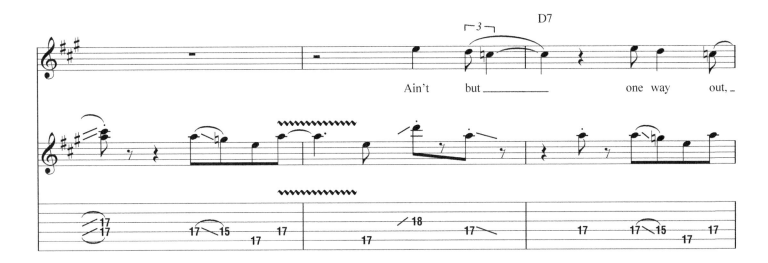

Ain't but _____ one way out, ___

___ ba - by.   and Lord, I   just___ can't go out that door.___

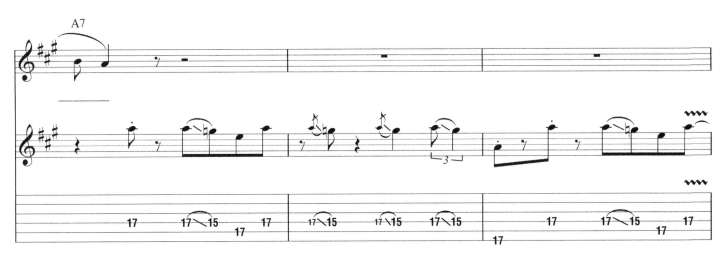

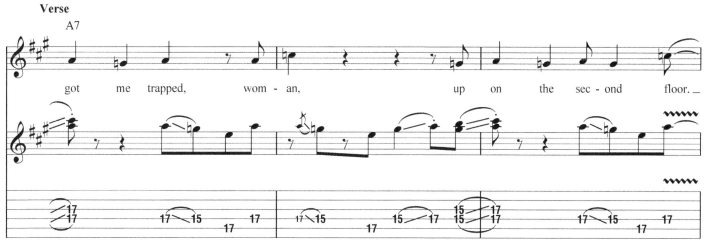

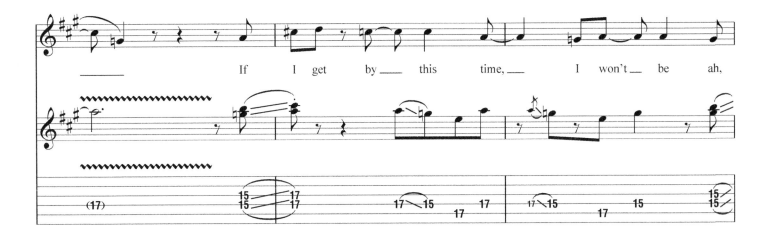

If I get by ___ this time, ___ I won't ___ be ah,

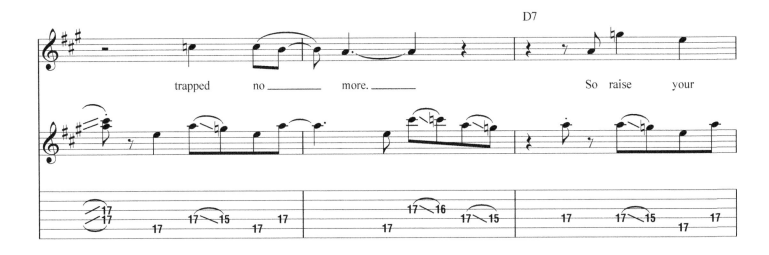

trapped no ___ more. ___ So raise your

win - dows, ba - by, I can ease ___ out soft ___ and

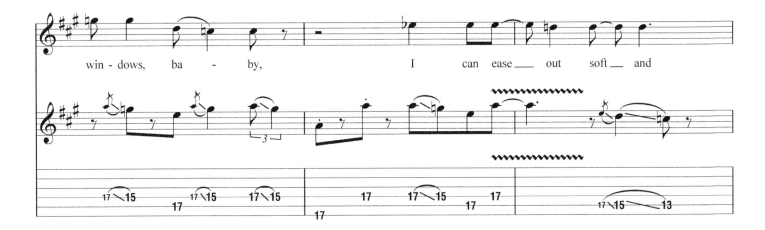

slow. ___

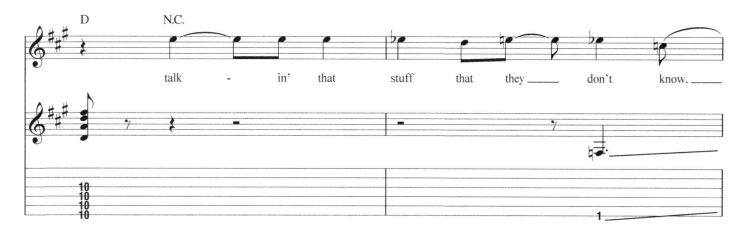

Guitar Solo

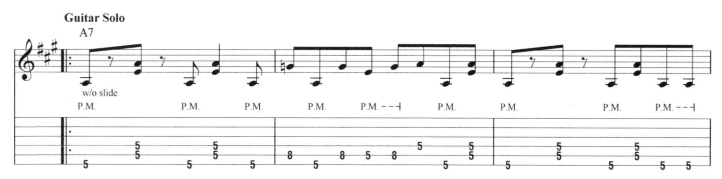

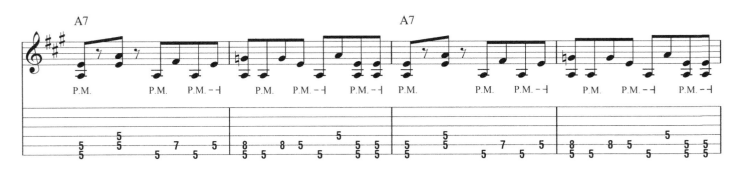

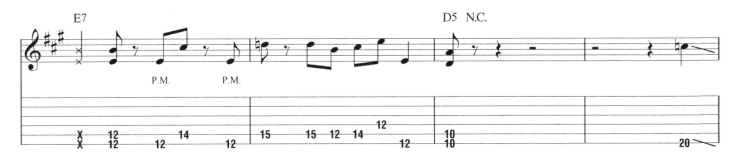

Drum Break

Guitar Solo

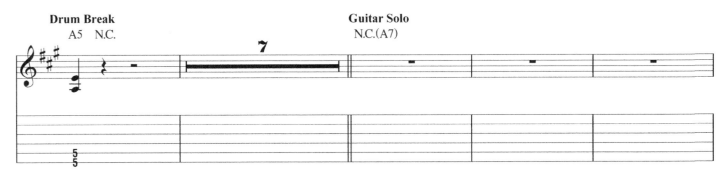

w/ slide

D7

8va

loco

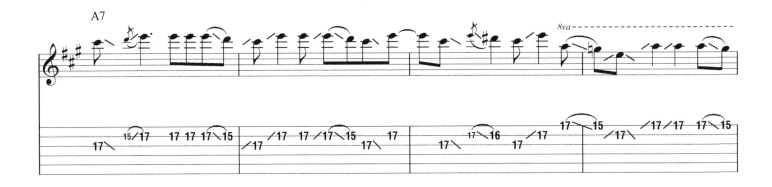

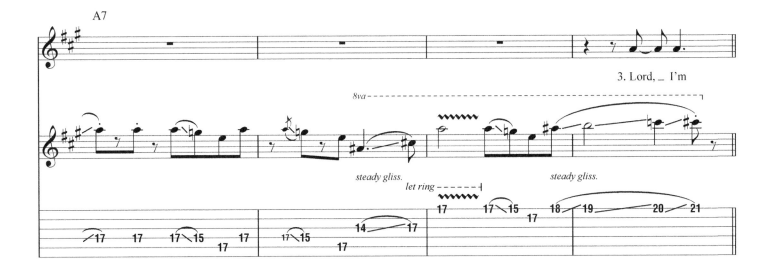

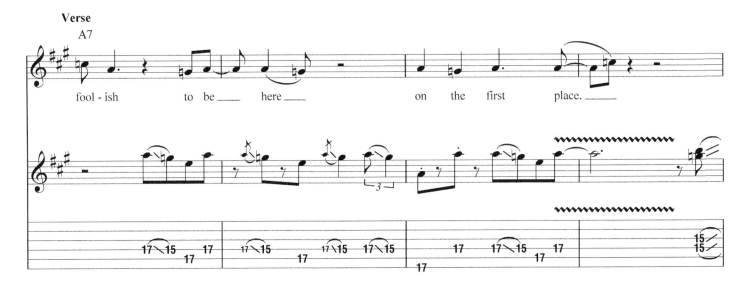

I know __ some man __ gon' walk __ in and   take   my _____ place.

Ain't no __   way   in   the   world _____   I'm   go- in' out __

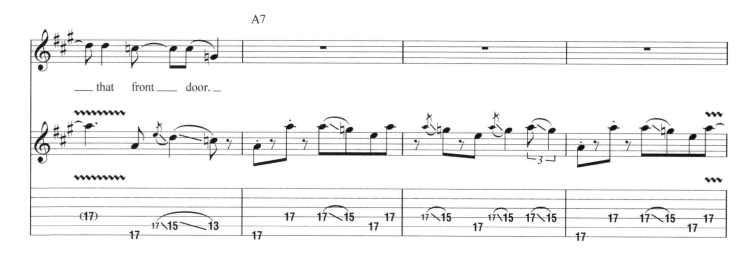

__ that   front __ door. __

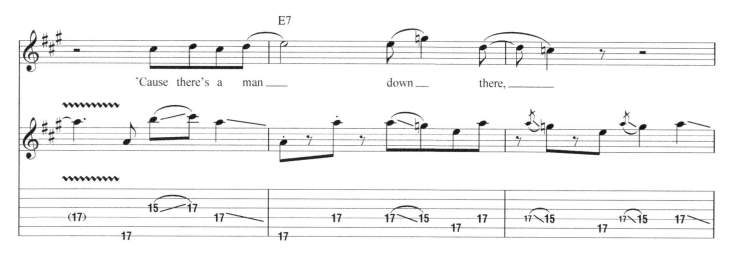

'Cause there's a   man __   down __   there, _____

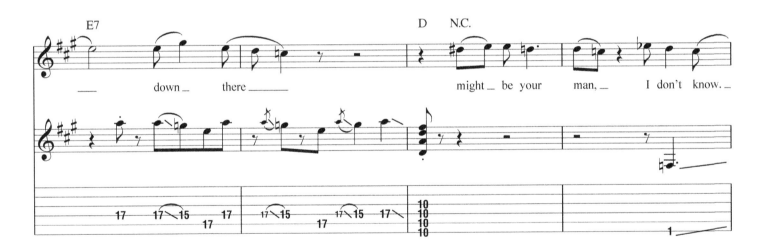

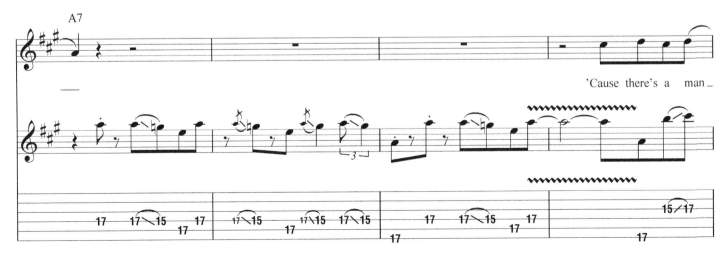

You Shook Me

Words and Music by Willie Dixon and J.B. Lenoir

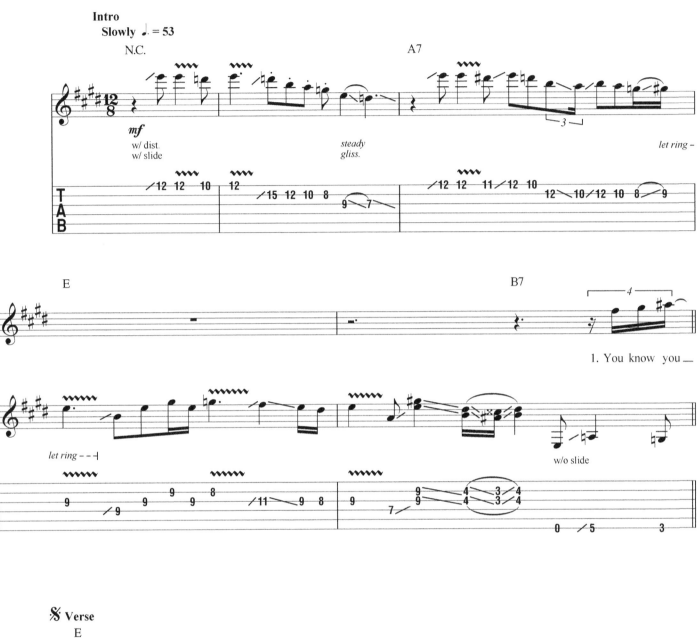

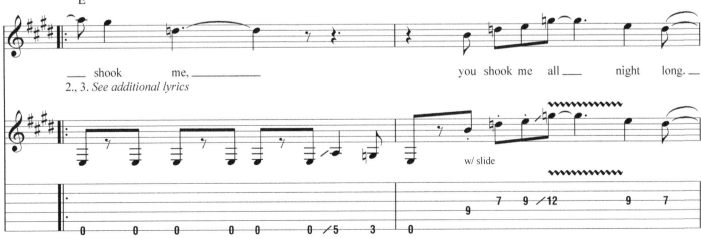

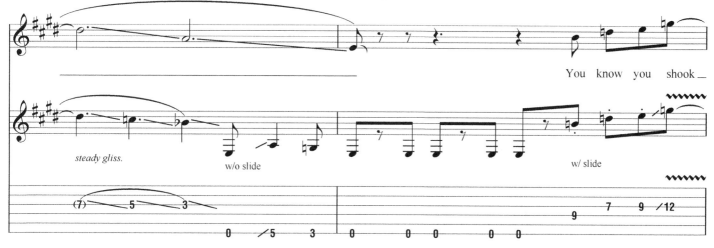

3rd time, substitute Fill 1

steady gliss.

w/o slide

w/ slide

You know you shook __

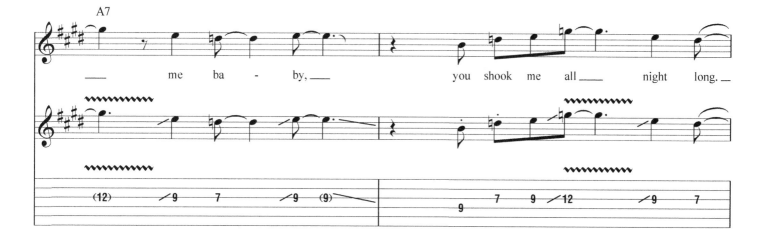

A7

__ me ba - by, ___ you shook me all ___ night long. ___

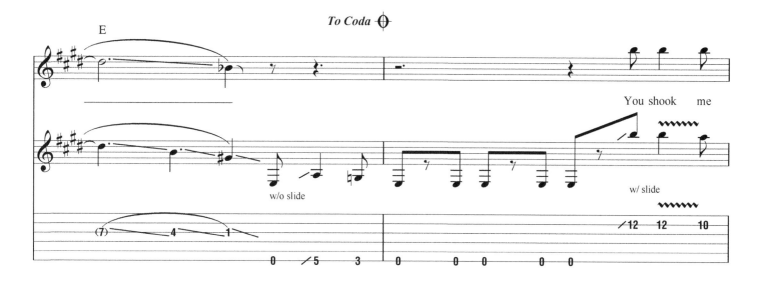

E

To Coda ⊕

You shook me

w/o slide

w/ slide

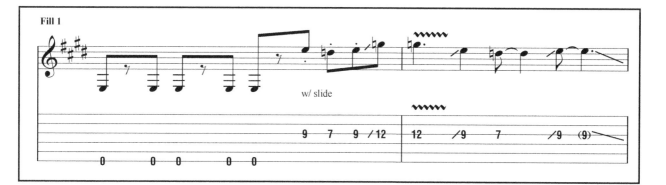

Fill 1

w/ slide

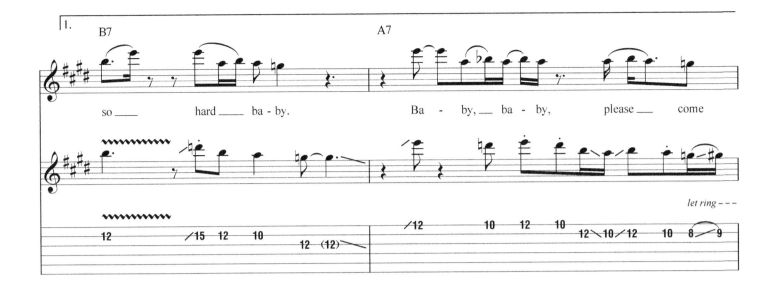

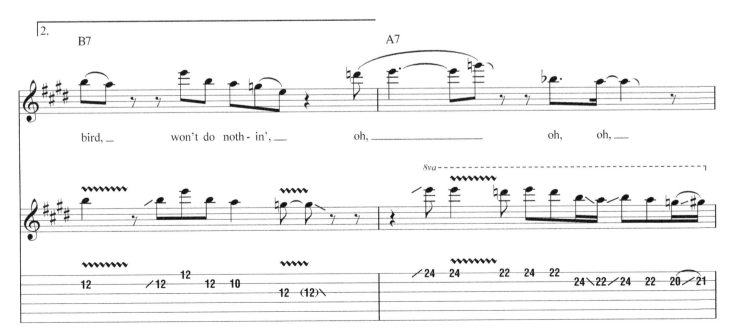

70

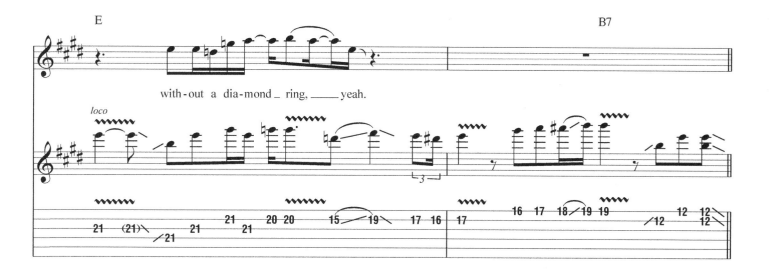

with-out a dia-mond ring, ____ yeah.

Organ Solo

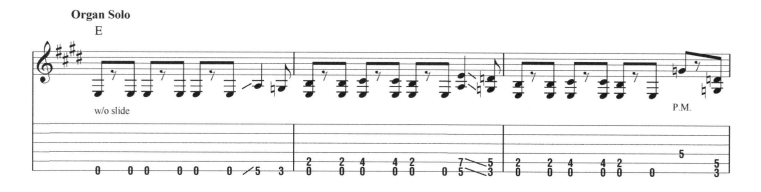

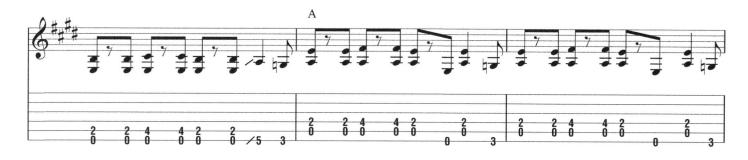

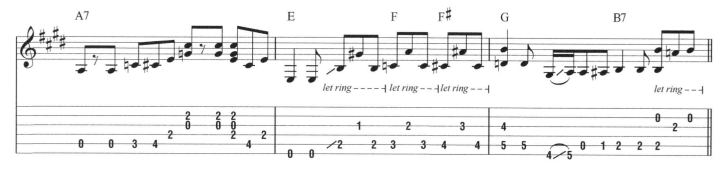

Harmonica Solo

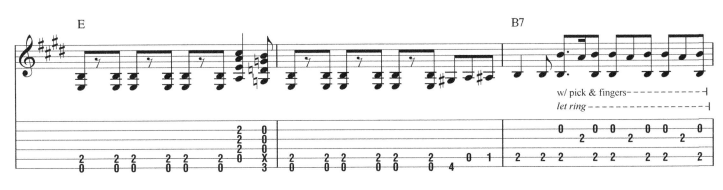

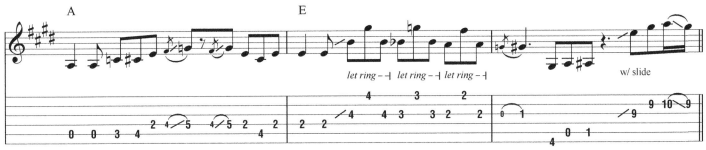

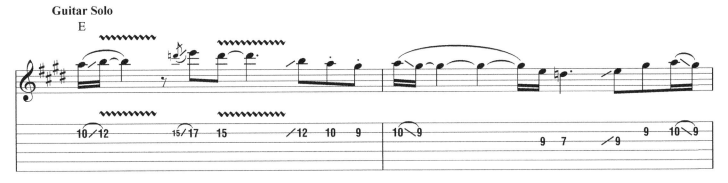

Guitar Solo

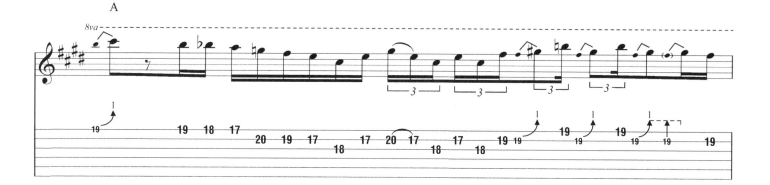

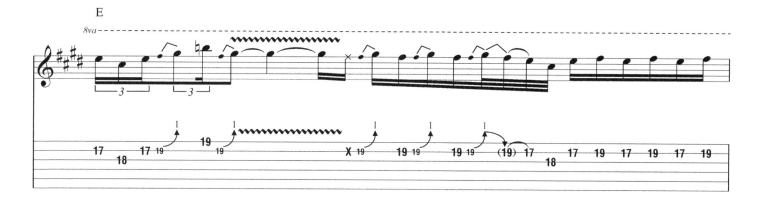

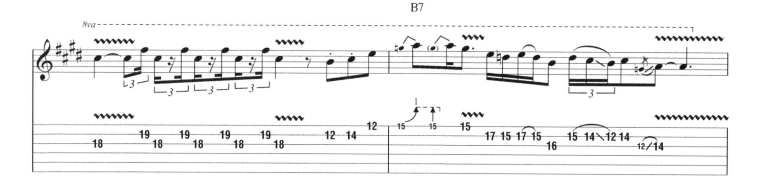

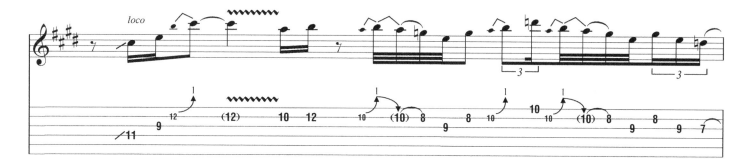

3. You know you

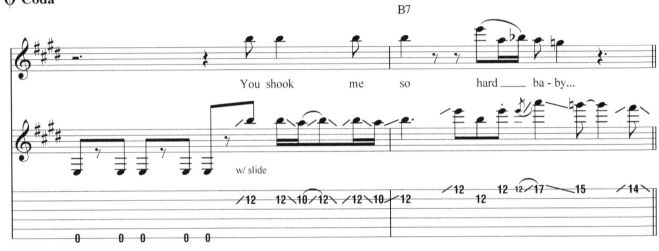

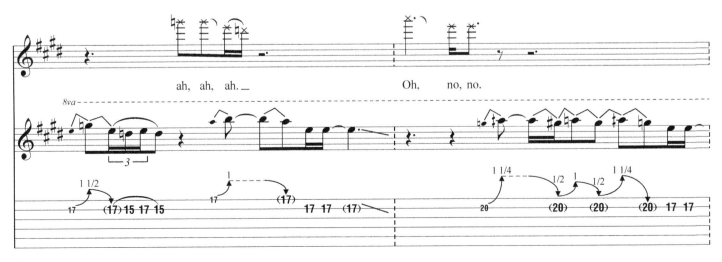

Additional Lyrics

2. I have a bird that whistles
   And I have birds that sing.
   I have a bird that whistles
   And I have birds that sing.
   I have a bird won't do nothin',
   Oh, oh, oh, without a diamond ring, yeah.

3. You know you shook me, babe,
   You shook me all night long.
   I know you really, really did babe.
   I think you shook me baby,
   You shook me all night long.
   You shook me so hard, baby...

Tush

Words and Music by Billy F Gibbons, Dusty Hill and Frank Lee Beard

Guitar Solo

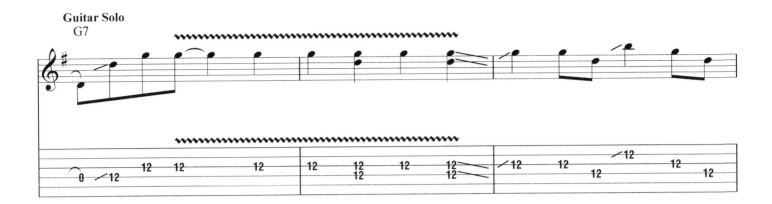

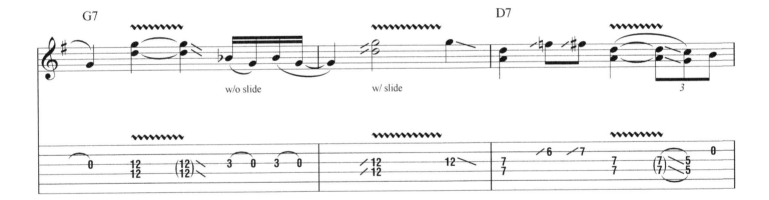

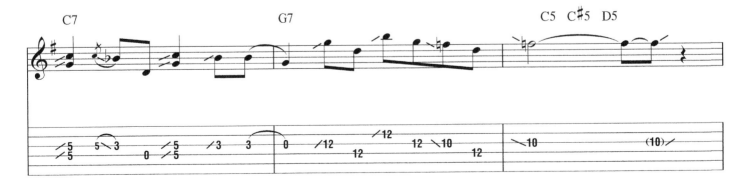

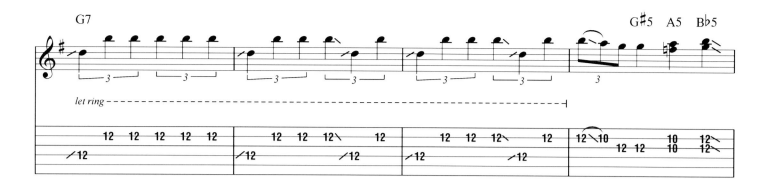

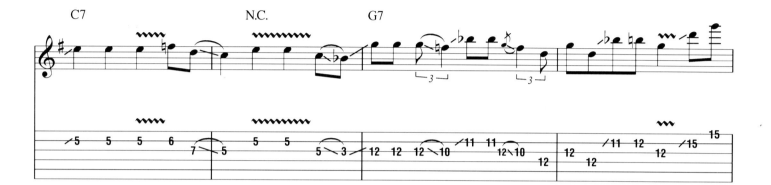

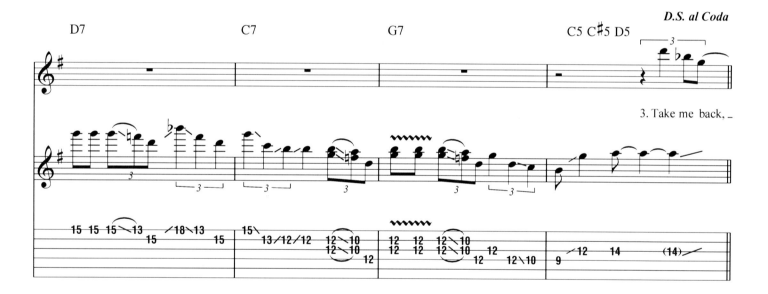

3. Take me back, _

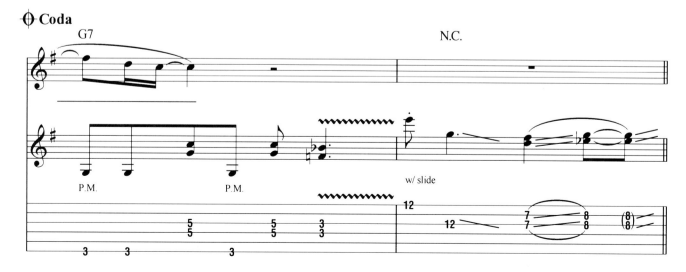

Outro-Guitar Solo

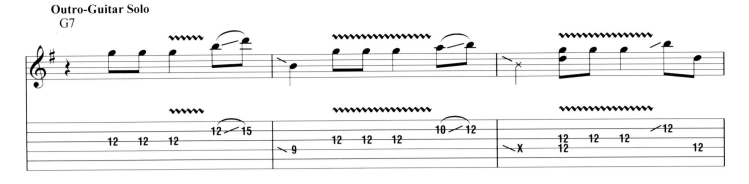

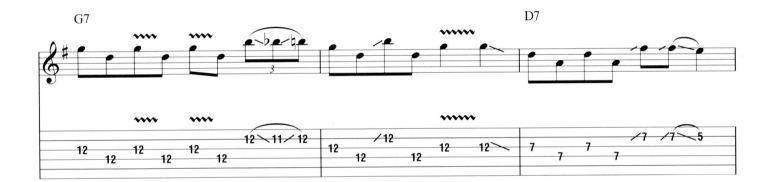

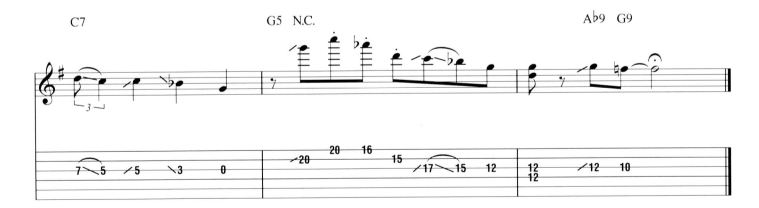

Additional Lyrics

2. I've been bad, I've been good,
   Dallas, Texas, Hollywood.
   I ain't askin' for much. Mm.
   I said, Lord, take me downtown.
   I'm just lookin' for some tush.

3. Take me back, way back home,
   Not by myself, not alone.
   I ain't askin' for much. Mm.
   I said, Lord, take me downtown.
   I'm just lookin' for some tush.